Jesus Calms
the St

Matthew 8:23–27
Mark 4:35–41
Luke 8:22–25
For Children
Written by Jean Thor Cook
Illustrated by Chris Wold Dyrud

ARCH® Books
Scripture quotations: NEW INTERNATIONAL VERSION® © 1973, 1978, 1984 by the International Bible Society.
Used by permission of Zondervan.

Copyright © 1994 Concordia Publishing House
3558 S. Jefferson Avenue, St. Louis, MO 63118-3968
Manufactured in the United States of America

Jesus was tired;
His hand covered a yawn.
The day had been busy,
From sunrise to sundown.

There'd been teaching and healing,
And stories to tell.
Many folks brought their sick,
And He made them well.

How could Jesus rest
With the crowd still there?
Why not sail 'cross the lake?
The disciples knew where.

The boat left the shore.
The crowd waved good-bye.
Jesus soon slept
Beneath the starry sky.

At first it was peaceful;
The waves splished and splashed.
But then a storm came up.
It came up so fast!

BANG! crashed the thunder.
It crackled, went *BOOM!*
Lightning zigzagged
And clouds hid the moon.

Jesus slept through it,
Cushion under His head—
Peaceful, relaxed,
As though in His bed.

The wind shrieked and moaned;
The boat gathered speed.
Why was Jesus sleeping?
His friends were in need!

"If this storm gets worse,"
They said with a cry,
"We'll have to wake Jesus,
Before we all die!"

The boat rose and fell;
The sea waved in lumps.
The men were so frightened—
They had big goose bumps!

They grabbed the boat's oars
And rowed with strong might.
The little boat groaned
In the black of the night.

The water rose higher.
The friends had one wish—
Knees knocking, they hoped
Not to swim with the fish.

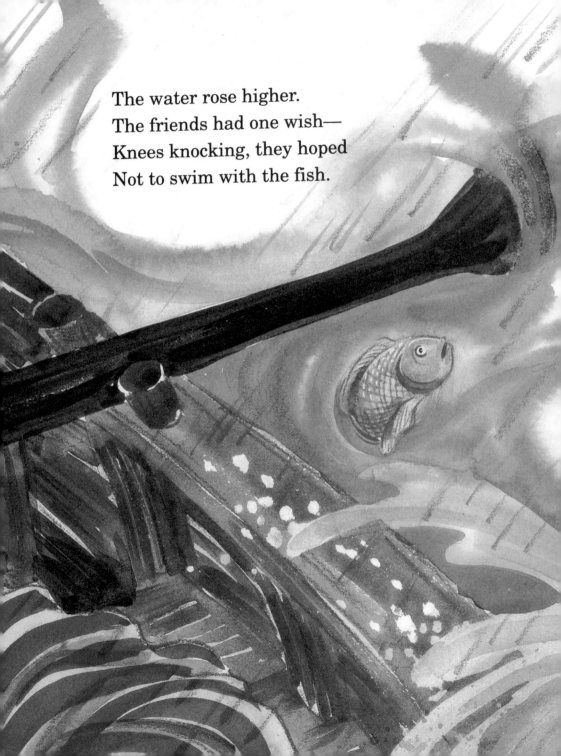

But the winds roared more fiercely.
Waves whooshed o'er the bow.
"We need to wake Jesus,
And do it right now!

"Don't you know we could perish?"
They questioned their Lord.
"Get up or we'll drown;
We'll be swept overboard!"

"Be quiet! Be still!"
Jesus spoke to the waves.
Quickly they calmed—
They had to obey.

Jesus asked His disciples,
"Why were you scared?
Have faith!" They'd forgotten—
Jesus always cared.

The disciples then wondered,
Who was this great man
Who brought them safe sailing,
Got them out of that jam?

He was awesome! Magnificent!
Full of power was He!
How did He take charge
Of those raging seas?

In time, they'd know Jesus
Was God's precious Son;
That His life would be given
To save everyone!

Dear Parents:

After reading this story, you might want to act it out by filling a pan with water. Sail a toy boat and blow on it with your child to create a storm. Then stop blowing and watch the storm end. Talk with your child about a time when you have been afraid. Help your child understand that we all feel afraid at times. Then read Psalm 56:3 together, "When I am afraid, I will trust in You."

Explain to your child that just as Jesus calmed the storm, He can calm our worries and fears and help us handle the problems that trouble us. He carried our greatest fear—fear of eternal death—to the cross and won our victory for us. Pray together with your child, thanking Jesus for His loving care.

The Editor